The Lucky Fishing Hat

Written by Jenny Feely

Illustrated by Chantal Stewart

Flying Start
to Literacy®

Contents

Chapter 1:
Gone fishing

"I'm going fishing," said Danny.
"The lake is covered in ice, but
I will cut a hole in the ice and catch
the biggest fish in the lake."

Danny got out all his fishing gear.
He put on his warmest clothes.

"I'm going to catch the biggest fish in the lake," said Ella as she put on a bright red hat.

"You can't fish in that hat," said Danny.

"Yes, I can. It's my lucky fishing hat," said Ella. "It will help me to catch the biggest fish. I am going to fish in this hat, and nothing you can say will stop me."

Chapter 2:
Ella's big catch

At the lake, Danny cut a hole in the ice. He put a worm on his hook and began to fish.

Ella also cut a hole in the ice. But before she began to fish, she waved her bright red hat over the fishing hole.

"Come to me, fish," she said.

"Hmmph!" said Danny.

In no time at all, Ella felt a tug
on her fishing line.

"I've got one," she said.

"How did you do that?" said Danny.

"Must be my lucky red hat," said Ella.
"The fish see it and they come to me."

"Hmmph," said Danny.

Ella hooked one fish after another.
Danny didn't catch anything.

Chapter 3:
Danger under the ice

Just as Danny was about to give up and go home, something gave a tug on his fishing line. It felt like a big, strong fish.

"Yippee," he yelled. "I've hooked the biggest fish in the lake."

But the fish pulled Danny off his feet and he began to slide into the fishing hole.

"Help!" he yelled.

Ella ran to help Danny, but she was too late. Danny slid into the hole and down into the water under the ice.

The big fish swam off, pulling Danny away from the fishing hole.

Danny let go of his fishing rod.

He looked around but he couldn't see the hole in the ice anywhere. The ice was a flat, dark sheet above him.

It was very cold under the ice.
Danny knew he had to get out quickly.

Chapter 4:
Ella's idea

Ella looked into the fishing hole.
She couldn't see Danny.

"He must be lost under the ice,"
she said. "I must help him to find
the fishing hole."

Ella tied her red hat to the end of
her fishing line and dropped it into
the fishing hole.

"Come to me, Danny. Look for the red fishing hat," she called.
The hat sank under the water.

Under the ice, Danny was getting colder and colder. He was almost out of breath. He couldn't see his fishing hole anywhere.

But then Danny saw something red. It was Ella's fishing hat tied to the end of her fishing line.

With his last bit of energy, Danny swam to the hat and held on tight. Then he gave it a tug.

Chapter 5:
A really big catch

Ella felt the tug, tug, tug on her line and she pulled and pulled and pulled.

Danny popped up out of the hole, holding her red fishing hat tightly in his hands.

"Your red fishing hat saved me!"
said Danny thankfully.

"See, I told you my red hat was lucky,"
said Ella.

A note from the author

This book owes its existence to my mother. She loves to go fishing with her brother – my uncle. The trouble is that she always wears very brightly coloured hats. When my uncle sees what she is wearing, he always says, "You can't go fishing in that hat!" My mother always replies, "But it's my lucky hat!" Every time she catches a fish, she says, "See, I told you it was lucky." This gave me the start of the story.

My mother is very proud that her fishing hats inspired me to write this book. She says that this means her hats are even luckier than she thought!